THE POEMS AND SONGS OF TALIESIN

JOHN MATTHEWS

APOCRYPHILE
PRESS

Apocryphile Press
PO Box 255
Hannacroix, NY 12087
www.apocryphilepress.com

Copyright © 2025 by John Matthews
Printed in the United States of America
ISBN 978-1-965646-45-8 | paper
ISBN 978-1-965646-46-5 | ePub

Cover art: 'Taliesin' by Miranda Grey, from *The Arthurian Tarot* by Caitlín and John Matthews.

No part of this book may be reproduced, stored in a retrieval system, or transmitted in any form or by any means—electronic, mechanical, photocopy, recording, or otherwise—without written permission of the author and publisher, except for brief quotations in printed reviews.

Please join our mailing list at www.apocryphilepress.com/free. We'll keep you up-to—date on all our new releases, and we'll also send you a FREE BOOK. Visit us today!

To Master T himself.

CONTENTS

Introduction	ix
The Figure of Taliesin	xiii
THE POEMS	1
1. The Song of Taliesin	2
2. Taliesin and the Doctrine of Intuition	5
3. Taliesin and the Rock	6
4. Taliesin and the River-Goddess	8
5. Taliesin and the Gulls	9
6. Taliesin in Winter	10
7. Taliesin at Merlin's Grave	12
8. Taliesin to the Night	14
9. Taliesin and the Salmon	15
10. Taliesin and the Spheres of the Planets	16
11. Taliesin and the Goddess	17
12. The Laughter of Taliesin	19
13. The Theory of Balance	20
14. Taliesin and the Dark	21
15. Taliesin and Morgain	22
16. Taliesin and the Fledgling Dream	23
17. Taliesin the Salmon	24
18. Taliesin Alone	26
19. Poem on Taliesin's Birthday	28
20. Taliesin and the Inspiration of Mother Earth	29
21. Taliesin and the Noble Head	30
22. Taliesin and the Stone of Seeing	31
23. Taliesin's Song of the Secrets	32
24. The King's Mind	34
25. Taliesin and the Burden of Love	35
26. Taliesin and Arthur	37
27. The Fall of the Kingdom	39
28. Taliesin's Creed	41
29. The Unicorn	43
30. Taliesin and the Night Hawk	45

31. The Reconciliation of Opposites	47
32. The Song of the Wind	49
33. The Lost Light	50
34. In Winter's Shadow	51
35. The Raid on Annwn	52
36. Taliesin's Song of the Apotheosis of Britain	55
37. Taliesin Sings the Heroes	57
38. The Voices in the Grass	60
39. Taliesin and the Silence of Winter	61
40. Taliesin and the Raven	63
41. Taliesin and the Song of the Quest	64
42. Taliesin and the Lake of Vision	66
43. Taliesin Enters the Wood	68
44. The Battles of Light and Dark	69
45. Taliesin and the Tree	71
46. Taliesin Sings of His Knowledge	72
47. Taliesin: The Poet's Eye	74
48. Taliesin's Quest	76
49. Taliesin's Madness	78
50. Song of the Grail-Lord	79
51. Taliesin to the Crows	81
52. Taliesin's Song of the Returning	83
53. Taliesin in the Moment	85
54. Taliesin the Shaman	86
55. Taliesin & the Song of Tradition	88
56. Taliesin's Lament for Llacheu the King's Son	90
57. Taliesin Sings the Mysteries	91
58. Taliesin Answers the Critics	93
59. A Song of the Empire	94
60. Before Camlann	98
61. Taliesin and the Nymph	100
62. Taliesin's Daemon	102
63. Taliesin and the Mingled Worlds of Christ	103
64. Taliesin Sees the Lovers Pass	105
65. Taliesin on the Thirteenth Stair	107
66. The Song of the Wind	109
67. Taliesin Dreams	110
68. Taliesin at the Weir	112
69. At the Weir Again	113

70. The Return of Taliesin	114
71. Taliesin and the World	115
72. A Chosen Death	116
73. The Last of the Wanderers	118
Further Reading	121

INTRODUCTION

Back in the mid 1960s I came across the poetry of Charles Williams (1886–1945), one of the loose-knit group of writers known as the Inklings, which included J.R.R. Tolkien and C.S. Lewis. I discovered Williams' two books of poems: *Taliessin through Logres* and *The Region of the Summer Stars* and devoured these extraordinary works, which delved deeply into Arthurian myth, already a central part of my own burgeoning work. Williams' powerful and mystical poetry focused on the figure of the 6th-century Welsh bard Taliesin, (whose name acquired an extra letter 's' in CW's writing). Concepts such as the world-forest of Broceliande and the empire of Byzantium which, for Williams, represented the world of the ancient Celts and the mystical strength of Christianity respectively, began to work their way into my own vision—to the extent that, looking back, I am astonished at how deeply Williams' work influenced my own at this time. Somehow, my research into the world of Arthur and the Round Table kept leading me back to Taliesin and I began to research the rich and complex material relating to this figure.

Little is known about this poet and singer, who lived in the 6th-century, perhaps in the same era as Arthur himself, but I

INTRODUCTION

quickly became acquainted with the poetry contained in one of the *Four Ancient Books of Wales* which bore his name. This led, in time, to my book *Taliesin: The Last Celtic Shaman (Inner Traditions, 2002)* which contained the first modern translations of his work, executed by myself and my wife.

The poems are rich in their references to the Celtic tradition, and though not all were composed by Taliesin himself, but rather attributed to him by the Christian monks who copied out the works from more ancient sources during the mediaeval period, they showed themselves to be part of an ancient tradition with its roots in the practise of shamanism in the early Celtic world.

I'm not sure when I wrote my first poem drawing upon this tradition, and was, I freely admit, influenced by Charles Williams' own work. My poetry at this time was evolving into an inner mythic landscape which it continues to occupy to this day, and the figure of Taliesin became a personal voice alongside my own—we seemed almost to be chorusing the words and images that began to emerge from my mind. I should add that I do not make any claim to possess the skill to match that of the great Welsh bard, or of Charles Williams, but I often feel that their presence has, throughout my life, influenced what I have written and the words I have chosen when writing them. These poems, in particular, and especially the earlier ones, dating back as far as the 1970s, seem to me to be less mine and more Taliesin's.

Since that time, I have produced almost a hundred poems which are either written in the voice of Taliesin himself or which reference him as a central figure. (My own—currently unfinished —novel, *Broceliande*, is told in the first person by Taliesin and draws heavily on the parallel myths of Logres—the ancient name for Arthur's Kingdom—and the mythology of Celtic Britain.) In 1991 I published a selection of stories, in parts derived from this ongoing epic, called *The Song of Taliesin* (Allen & Unwin), which included, between each story, some of the poems I had composed at this point.

INTRODUCTION

Over the years I have continued to read and study Charles Williams' work, and my own 'Taliesin' poems are still happening. In 2022 I was invited to co-edit and collect all of Williams' published Arthurian poems into a single volume. Working with Grevel Lindop, the author of the only full length biography of Williams, we assembled some of his earliest work alongside the mature development which continued to evolve until his untimely death in 1945. (*The Arthurian Poems of Charles Williams: Including Taliessin Through Logres and The Region of the Summer Stars with Other Poems*)

Writing an introductory essay on the world of Arthur and Taliesin, I found myself looking back at my own work, and was astonished at how much my own compositions had been influenced by both Williams and the original poems of Taliesin. The present collection represents what I feel to be the best of these. Not every one is included, but some were 'outliers' that I felt did not belong with the core of what I began to see as a sequence of work. There is, indeed, a kind of story to be found within these works, but it is not a sequential one, but rather, glimpses seen amid the trees of the Great Wood. I am enormously grateful to John Mabry, my publisher, for suggesting that I gather these works into a volume for the first time, and for his continuing enthusiasm for my work as a whole, and for these in particular.

For those unfamiliar with the traditions of Taliesin, I have included an introductory essay; for further information and translations of his extent works, I refer my readers to my previous book, *Taliesin the Last Celtic Shaman*. I have also provided a few minor notes to the less familiar aspects of the Arthurian world, which has dominated almost everything I have written throughout my life. I have no doubt that there will be more 'Taliesin' poems to come, but for now this collection brings together all that I feel worthy of preserving. As Charles Williams himself wrote, in the prelude to his currently unpublished early work *The Advent of Galahad*, referencing the quest for the Grail:

INTRODUCTION

*'happy they who one song can add
of the quest of our Lord Dom Galahad.'*

John Matthews
Oxford
8th of August 2025

THE FIGURE OF TALIESIN

Most of what we know about the remarkable figure of Taliesin comes from two sources: a 16th-century text called the *Hanes* or 'Life' of Taliesin; and the 70 poems contained in a 14th-century volume known as *The Book of Taliesin*, one of the *Four Ancient Books of Wales*. Apart from these there are some references in the *Mabinogion* story of 'Branwen Daughter of Llyr' and a list of famous living bards contained in the writings of the 6th-century monk Nennius which includes Taliesin as amongst the greatest poets in the land.

These works date Taliesin to the 6th-century AD and this is supported by historical references in the poems themselves. However, although the mere fact of Taliesin's historical existence is fascinating and could lead us into some interesting areas, I want to concentrate on another Taliesin: a semi-mythical figure who is made up of a ragbag of references to and memories of things that happened far earlier than the 6th-century—things in fact that date back to the mists of antiquity, when the links between the earth and the people who lived upon it were more profound and real than at any time since. It is not, of course, a precise historical time, but more of a semi-mythical period when magic was taken as a matter of course and when almost anything could happen and probably did.

Not that Taliesin lived then. The truth is that he is the inheritor of many of the beliefs of that time—a focus, one might say, for all the memories that were still locked in the unconscious minds of the people who lived in these lands, both during the 6th-century and among those who were still half-conscious of a more primitive self as late as the 16th, when the literary mind of a Welsh writer named Llewellyn Sion, wrote down the text of the *Hanes Taliesin*. This takes us directly into the magical world* of the *Mabinogion*, which, as one of its translators put it: 'probably dates back to the dawn of the Celtic world.'

Not only the Celtic world however. The foundations on which these stories (especially Taliesin's) rest are both older and wider than any single culture. Here is just the first half of the story as it appears in the *Hanes*.

> In the time of Arthur there lived in the region of Llyn Tegid [Bala Lake] a nobleman named Tegid Voel [the Bald]. And he had a wife who was named Ceridwen, who was skilled in the magical arts. Tegid and Ceridwen had two children: one who was so ugly that they called him Morfran 'Great Crow,' but who came to be known as Afagddu 'Utter Darkness,' because of his extreme ugliness. The Other child was a daughter, whose name was Creirwy (Dear One) and she was as fair as Morfran was dark. Ceridwen thought that her son would never be accepted in the world because of his hideous looks, so she cast about for a way to empower him with wisdom, so that none would care about his appearance. And so she resolved to boil a Cauldron of Inspiration and Wisdom according to the Books of the Fferyllt, and the method of it was this: She must first gather certain herbs on certain days and hours, and put them in the Cauldron,

---

* P.K.Ford: *The Mabinogion and Other Medieval Welsh Tales*. University of California, 1977.

which must then be kept boiling for a year and a day, until three drops of Inspiration were obtained. For the task of maintaining the fire beneath the Cauldron Ceridwen chose an old blind man named Morda, who was led by a youth named Gwion Bach [Little], the son of Gwreang of Llanfair Caereinion in Powys.

At the end of the year Ceridwen stationed herself, with her son, close by the Cauldron, and there she fell asleep. And while she slept it happened that three drops flew out of the Cauldron and landed on the thumb of Gwion Bach, and so great was the pain that he put his thumb into his mouth and sucked it. And at once he knew all that there was to know, and foremost of that knowledge was that Ceridwen would destroy him as soon as she learned what had happened. And thus he fled. But the Cauldron gave a great cry, and cracked in two, and the waters flowed from it into a nearby stream and poisoned the horses of Gwyddno Garanhir. And Ceridwen awoke and when she saw what had occurred her anger knew no bounds. She struck the blind Morda so hard that one of his eyes fell out on his cheek, but he said that she had injured him wrongly. Then Ceridwen knew all that had occurred and went in pursuit of Gwion, running. And he was aware of her and changed himself into the semblance of a hare; and she, perceiving that, turned herself into the semblance of a black greyhound. He ran to a river and became a fish; and she pursued him as an otter-bitch, until he turned himself into a bird of the air and she into a hawk. Then, in fear for his life, he saw where a heap of winnowed wheat lay on the floor of a barn, and dropping amongst them, turned himself into one of the grains. Then Ceridwen turned herself into a black, red-crested hen and swallowed the grain of wheat, which went into her womb, so that she became quickened and bore Gwion in her womb for nine months. And when she gave birth to him he was so fair and beautiful that she could not bear to kill him, or to have another kill him for her. And so she placed him in a leather bag and set him adrift on the sea on the 29th day of April [or on Calen Gaef, the 31st of October].

Now there lived at that time, in the lordship of Maelgwn Gwynedd, a nobleman named Gwyddno Garanhir. He had a weir on the shore of the river Conwy, between Dyvi and Aberystwyth, close to the sea. And on every May Eve he was accustomed to take from it salmon to the value of a hundred pounds. And Gwyddno had one son who was named Elffin, a hapless youth who had nothing but evil luck. Therefore his father told him that on this particular year he should have all that he could find in the weir. So Elffin went to the weir on May Eve and when he and his servants arrived they could see that there was not so much as a single salmon in the nets. Then Elffin began to lament, until one of the men with him pointed out where a leather bag hung upon a pole of the weir. Then Elffin took the bag from the water and cut a slit in it with his knife. And within he saw a bright forehead and cried aloud: 'Behold, a radiant brow' (tal-iesin). And the child within the bag replied: 'Tal-iesin it is!' Thereupon Elffin took the child up and placed it before him on the crupper of his saddle and rode for home. And as he rode the child made a poem for him, which was 'The Consolation of Elffin'

Fair Elffin, cease your sorrow!
  Swearing profits no-one.
  It is not evil to hope,
  Nor does any man see what supports him,
  Not an empty treasure is the prayer of Cynllo,
  Nor does God break his promise.
  No catch in Gwyddno's weir
  Was ever as good as tonight's.

Fair Elffin, dry your cheeks!
  Such sorrow does not become you,
  Although you thought yourself cheated
  Excessive sorrow gains nothing,
  Nor will doubting God's miracles.

Although I am small, I am skilful.
From the sea and the mountain,
From the river's depth
God gives his gifts to the blessed

Elffin of the generous custom,
 Cowardly is your purpose,
 You must not grieve so heavily.
 Better are good than evil omens.
 Though I am weak and small,
 Spumed with Dylan's wave,
 I shall be better for you
 Than three hundred shares of salmon.

Elffin of noble generosity,
 Do not sorrow at your catch.
 Though I am weak on the floor of my basket,
 There are wonders on my tongue.
 While I am watching over you,
 No great need will overcome you.

It is told that this was the first poem that Taliesin made. And Elffin was filled with wonder, and asked the child how he came to compose poetry, and he so young; and Taliesin replied with another poem, which is called 'The Life of Taliesin' and by the time he had sung it they were back at Gwyddno's court.

Firstly I was formed in the shape of a handsome man,
 in the hall of Ceridwen in order to be refined.
 Although small and modest in my behaviour,
 I was great in her lofty sanctuary.

While I was held prisoner, sweet inspiration educated me
 and laws were imparted me in a speech which had no words;
 but I had to flee from the angry, terrible hag

whose outcry was terrifying.

Since then I have fled in the shape of a crow,
since then I have fled as a speedy frog,
since then I have fled with rage in my chains,
—a roebuck in a dense thicket.

I have fled in the shape of a raven of prophetic speech,
in the shape of satirizing fox,
in the shape of a sure swift,
in the shape of a squirrel vainly hiding.

I have fled in the shape of a red deer,
in the shape of iron in a fierce fire,
in the shape of a sword sowing death and disaster,
in the shape of a bull, relentlessly struggling.

I have fled in the shape of a bristly boar in a ravine,
in the shape of a grain of wheat.
I have been taken by the talons of a bird of prey
which increased until it took the size of a foal.

Floating like a boat in its waters,
I was thrown into a dark bag,
and on an endless sea, I was set adrift.

Just as I was suffocating, I had a happy omen,
and the Master of the Heavens brought me to liberty.
—translation by Caitlín Matthews

Here we have two of the many poems attributed to Taliesin —quite different to my own, but perhaps suggesting links between them. What does this tell us about Taliesin? It says, quite clearly, that he was one of the Wondrous Children who appear regularly in Celtic myth, and who include Fionn

MacCumhail, Pwyll, Pryderi, Gwair, Goreu, and the child god Mabon.

Once Taliesin is ensconced in Elffin's home he demonstrates his powers as a prophet and makes some extraordinary claims to have been in many places and times throughout history. These boasts are echoed throughout much of the poetry of the period. We may view these statements as elliptical references to a certain kind of inner knowledge. It is most clearly indicated by the *Hanes* account of Taliesin's rebirth. This whole episode is both a mishmash of stories from very ancient Celtic belief systems as well as a clear description of an initiation.

This is all in line with my belief that Taliesin is a repository for an age-old tradition, shared in part by all initiates. We can learn more of Taliesin's particular role from another poem from *The Book of Taliesin*, which has become his best-known work. This is the *Prieddeu Annwfn* or 'Raid on Annwn,' the Celtic Otherworld, in search of a cauldron with special properties and which relates to the Cauldron of Ceridwen from which Taliesin received his own wisdom.

Prieddeu Annwn adds further details. It is a difficult text to unravel, but here are some extracts to give an idea of its complexity and mystery.

> *Predestined was Gweir's captivity in Caer Sidi,*
>   *According to the tale of Pwyll and Pryderi.*
> *None before him was sent into it,*
> *Into the heavy blue chain which bound the youth.*
> *From before the reeving of Annwfn he has groaned,*
> *Until the ending of the world this prayer of poets:*
> *Three ship burdens of Prydwen entered the Spiral City*
> *Except seven, none returned from Caer Sidi.*

> *Is not my song worthily to be heard*
>   *In the four-square Caer, four times revolving!*
> *I draw my knowledge from the famous cauldron,*

The breath of nine maidens keeps it boiling.
Is not the Head of Annwfn's cauldron so shaped:
Ridged with enamel, rimmed with pearl?
It will not boil the cowardly traitor's portion.
The sword of Lleawc flashed before it
And in the hand of Lleminawc was it wielded.
Before hell's gate the lights were lifted
When with Arthur we went to the harrowing.
Except seven none returned from Caer Feddwit.
—*translation by Caitlín Matthews*

This is all most mysterious and repays much study and meditation. For the moment we should notice the references to the imprisoned youth, Gwair, the Cauldron warmed by the breath of nine muses, the visits to the seven mysterious Caers, and of course the fact that Taliesin is among the seven who return from the voyage.

One possible explanation of this curious text may be found in the *Story of Branwen* from the *Mabinogion*, which is also about a mysterious Cauldron. Bran, who is a god-like figure, possesses a wondrous vessel that has the property of bringing the dead to life when they are placed within it—though they come forth dumb and unable to speak of what they have seen. When one of Bran's brothers, Evnissien, causes insult to the King of Ireland, Bran gives him, by way of recompense, this same cauldron, which had, in fact originally come from Ireland. The story of its discovery is especially interesting.

> One day when Matholwch, the King of Ireland, was hunting near the Lake of the Cauldron, he saw a huge yellow-haired man coming from the Lake with a cauldron on his back. A woman followed him, who was also of great size. And because she was with child and the couple had nowhere to live, Matholwch invited them to return with him to his court. He soon regretted this, because the woman gave birth not to one child but to

hundreds—one every month in fact, and every one a fully armed warrior. Needless to say this made them very unpopular, especially as their general behaviour was also terrible. Matholwch soon tried to get rid of them, having a specially built house prepared, made of iron, which was sealed as soon as the couple entered and its walls heated until they glowed white. But the terrible couple broke out and fled, taking the Cauldron with them. When they arrived in Britain, Bran received them using the woman's seemingly endless reproductive ability to garrison fortresses all over the land. Later on in the same story, when Bran and Matholwch are in conflict, the Irish use the Cauldron to restore their dead warriors, and it is only finally broken when Evnissien, who had caused all the trouble to begin with, crawls inside and stretches himself out, killing himself in the process. Of that fateful war only seven men escaped, including Taliesin.

If we look beneath the surface of this story it can be used to explain a number of things from both the *Prieddeu Annwn* and the *Hanes Taliesin*. Although the giant couple are called by other names in the Branwen text, they are clearly reflections of Tegid Voel and his wife Ceridwen. She herself was originally a goddess of gestation and birth, a Mountain Mother who in some stories is seen as letting fall from her skirt great stones that become mountains and hills.

The endless stream of warriors born by her confirm this identification, and it is perhaps possible to see the Cauldron itself as a symbolic womb—from which not only is life given, but also knowledge, wisdom, the *awen* or inspiration of the Poet. When the Cauldron is in the hands of other men, they are unable to create life, only restore those who were dead.

It is also clear that at some stage in the transmission of the various tales which went into the making of Branwen the original story concerned a voyage to capture the fabled cauldron of Rebirth and Inspiration, and that Taliesin, as an initiate of its secrets, not only accompanied them but was one of the seven—a mystic number—who returned from the Otherworld to tell the tale.

Taliesin is, then, someone who has access to the kind of knowledge which enables him to travel and return from the Otherworld. He experiences self-induced trances that give him insight into events both past and future. He is closely connected with a probable cult of initiates who traced their source of inspiration to the Goddess Ceridwen, the same who was the possessor of a cauldron from which Taliesin was said to have been reborn. He thus resembles in several points the figure of the shaman, who also had the ability to visit the otherworld, had visions of past and future, and underwent various forms of initiation in which they were 'reborn' with extended powers and deepened knowledge. Seen in this light the story of Taliesin falls into place. It is an account of a poetic, even a shamanic, initiation that gives whoever experiences it access to perception outside the ordinary.

This is part of the background to the poems collected here. For a full exploration of the Taliesin story and translations of the poetry attributed to him, see my *Taliesin: The Last Celtic Shaman* (Inner Traditions, 2002.)

—John Matthews, Oxford, 2025

THE POEMS

I

THE SONG OF TALIESIN

I have been
from the beginning.
I have seen
all manner of things.
My voice has been heard
upraised in song,
in the halls of kings,
in the palaces of princes,
in the houses of people,
in the groves of the Druid.
And I have sung,
let all men believe it,
before the Chair of the Sovereign,
Arthur the Blessed,
who drove all before him,
who stood at the gate of Annwn
with sword in hand
and brought forth the Hallows,
the four holy objects,
for the blessing of the Land.
I have stood on the walls

of the turning fortress.
I have dwelt three times
in the womb of the Goddess.
Bard am I,
Taliesin the singer.
I have spoken with Merlin
in his habitations of glass.
I have drunk of the awen,
from the Cauldron of Inspiration,
nine nights and days
in the womb of Ceridwen.
From that day,
I have travelled the wide world.
I have stood upon the walls
of Troia the golden.
I have watched over battles
in the forefront of the host.
I have stood in the place
where the Son of Man was laid;
I have spoken to Magi
in the groves of Avaron;
I have walked all roads
between Eryri and Emmaeus;
I have heard the words
of the wisest of the wise;
I have sung to princes
in the halls of Byzantium;
I have chanted my words
before the Lords of Hosts.
Who I was
remains unknown.
In time men shall call me
Merlin and Jokannan.
Three times imprisoned
in the place of the Goddess

I still am enclosed
in the circle of the world.
In the pattern of creation
I seek my source,
in the tremendous force
of the Holy Word.
In the dreaming of choirs
of the mighty abbey,
in the halls of Lordship
and the halls of Death.
I adore the splendor
and the majesty of Fortune.
In the region of the Summer Stars
I find my beginning;
in the Circle of Abred[*]
I observe my end.
Until that moment
in the turning spheres,
I continue my story
until called to cease.

My time will remain
in the thoughts of all,
until I enter the region
where I find my home.

---

[*] The first circle of existence in Druidic lore, in which are all corporal and dead existences.

2
TALIESIN AND THE DOCTRINE OF INTUITION

Taliesin lay in earth,
His birth far distant as the sun.
But his mind stretched out
To touch the shut lids of time.
He became his own god,
Bled life into the world.
Rivers flowed through his veins,
His breath assumed the power of winds.

Moon and Sun glittered from his eyes.
He offered his breast to the greedy mouth of time,
His body to the lusts of earth.
Present at the birth of stars,
Their nature and kind he saw foreshadowed,
And from their essence was created god.
Now on his bed of earth he turned
And began again the journey toward birth.

3
TALIESIN AND THE ROCK

Taliesin felt his way into the rock.
He fingered the dark holes of its brain.
His hands and encountered the dark.
He touched life.
His eyes saw with the sight of the rock.
He breathed with the breath of the rock.
His fingers the wind touched,
His feet the sea washed.
His thought lay in the head of the rock:
Tintagel gripping the White Brow.
His sweat ran in streams down the face of rock.
He mingled with sea salt and sea mist.
He blew out on the wind's back.
The sky swallowed his heart.
He beat with the tick
     of the beating world.
         He beat.
The wind shook his hair.
The sand formed itself to a pattern
Of the Iron Crown, spiked and spurred.
His fingers forgot they were fingers.

His body forgot all it had remembered.
He learned the secret of the birth of rock.
A seabird without wings he swept
Into the sky and through the sky—
Air rocked with wings.
In the cave his fingers and feet
Released rock. Strands of hair
Twisted in the water and the air.

4
TALIESIN AND THE RIVER-GODDESS

Taliesin walked by the riverbank.
A Kingfisher flashed downstream,
And like a wave the River-Goddess rose.
Hair like green gold hung around her face,
Her breasts were the ripest moons.
She smiled at the Poet as he stood
Watching her like a dark bird.
She said: 'The river believes in itself;
The poet only in his own cold dream.'
She raised her arms and beckoned him.
Taliesin smiled, lifting his left hand.
The river raged suddenly between its banks
And the Goddess was veiled in spray.
Water splashed to the poet's feet.
Smiling he walked away.

5
TALIESIN AND THE GULLS

Taliesin walked by the shore.
The cries of gulls flashed in his ears.
The sea sound thundered in his brain.
The lips of the Poet grew stiff and frozen.
His song, through scraped bone,
Rattled in his throat.
Released, it rode above the wave tops.
Birds poured back from his eyes.
He watched them fly: flew with them:
Swept in spirals.
Birds flowed and ebbed around him.
Shadows eddied on the white sand.
Swift and smooth his thoughts flew.
His bones cracked in bright air.
Out of the blue circle, pierced with gold,
The Poet flew where his feet had walked.
Sunlight flashed on broken waters.
The sea sound crept in his brain.

6
TALIESIN IN WINTER

Under the broad brow of winter
the poet hunched, staring out
at the black branches
of the starving wood,
his breath a white fog
from which words formed:

'O Goddess of the cold and ice
I surrender to your touch,
melting down into darkness
under the earth,
where stars shine nonetheless,
and where, in the breath between
one winter and the next
I find a message written.'

He waited in the shelter of standing stones
and in his hands and feet
touched the pain of snow-bent boughs.
His eyes were the colour of frost.
The melting snow flowed from him.

TALIESIN IN WINTER

His voice thawed.
He barked like a fox at midnight
who sang with the water's release.
His eyes were the colour of spray

Sent forth, the poet danced,
making bird prints in the white
unvarying snowfields where
he found certain answers
not even he could utter.

TALIESIN AT MERLIN'S GRAVE

The voice of Merlin sang
From the depths of the Earth:

'To have been present
At the birth of worlds,
To have set free the beast
Which tears at the throat of life—
No terror could be this great,
Unless it might be
The flash of the Goddess' hand
Flinging words like knives into the mind.

'There were poems written before this,
Written out of the agony of stone and stem,
Broken from the flesh like flakes of bone;
Dreams given flesh by feeling—
The secret children of desire,
With only the soundless stars
To view their primogeniture.
Now you are come here, poet, singer,
To this place of stones.

And what can you do save hunger
For the long waking dream of death.'

The poet turned away into the shredding mist
preparing his secret road towards the light,
leaving the seer to his ancient rest.

8
TALIESIN TO THE NIGHT

Taliesin whispered words in the ear of night.
He spoke of stones, the river, silence.
He received back the imprint of his truth.
Soft-footed, he ranged the night-palled hills
Murmuring his song to a dark and empty sky.
In the endlessly repeated call of a fenland bird
He heard and understood the meaning of his life.

9
TALIESIN AND THE SALMON

Taliesin walked in the Silent Wood.
Where the sunlight struck deep,
like a sword plunged in Moss,
he halted, bent above the pool.
'Salmon of Wisdom,' he murmured,
'Today I saw One walking
whose breath became my breath,
whose hand brushed mine
like a fiery kiss; who left
a trail of scattered stars glinting in the grass;
and when I looked, wore on her brows
a jewel of undying brilliance.'
He looked into the water, saw
the speckled body lazily drift
into the race that carried it downstream.
In its own time it would answer.
Meanwhile he had the Mystery to play.

10

TALIESIN AND THE SPHERES OF THE PLANETS

Taliesin heard the music of the spheres.
He spoke from age to age,
Seeing how each life was marked
By its place in the pattern of the stars.
Under their light he found
The places of the gods,
Saw them fallen or dead.
He looked for, and found, the King's Shadow
Stretching from Aquarius to Mars.
Sighing, the Poet traced his Lord's destiny
From the double birth of Gemini
To his rising in the Lunar East.

II
TALIESIN AND THE GODDESS

Taliesin weighed his thoughts
And smiled, thinking of love.
'No part has it in the patterns I lay
Of small stones along the shore—
The maze I walk,
Too fragile to withstand my touch.'
He looked across the spaces of the court,
And saw, like a white bird at first,
A figure: tall, striding, her face
Turned half from him, lips drawn back
From white sharp teeth.

She passes in a held breath.
Released into movement he crossed the court,
Stood upon the walls looking forth
Across winter lands
Breaking into spring beneath his sight.
To the sky and wheeling birds he sang:
'Softly walks the mistress of the Winding Way;
Forgives me if I do not bow; lets it be enough

That I have taken breath,
Trembled in the chill of her passing.'

He smiled and raised his hands.
Far away the lightning flickered
Like white birds on the castle's rim.

12
THE LAUGHTER OF TALIESIN

In the shadow of the walls Taliesin
Touched the strings of his harp.
The Dream sang in his skull
Like a nightingale in summer.
Raising his eyes he stared
Through walls of stone
To where the thorntree battled with the wind.

'No song,' he murmured, 'rises in me tonight;
Though I continue to challenge the spirit of the trees.'
Laughter bubbled in his throat, scattering his words;
He raised his cup and drained it to the depth—
And in the dregs of wine saw mirrored
The tall-cliffed island and its glassy tower,
And heard the wind howl darkly through the trees.

His laughter grew to a sudden shout
Scattering the birds on the castle roof.
The walls wavered in a sudden draught of song—
While beyond their transparency, the daylight broke.

13
THE THEORY OF BALANCE

Waves struck the shore like hammer blows,
beating out the metre of his thought.
The wind groaned in the whale's rib
and the long-drawn notes of song
subtly chimed in the Poet's brain.
Standing on a knife-ridge of rock
he stared at frail clusters of moss,
balance lightly on the edge
of knowledge and time.
He saw all things equally,
and neither accepted nor denied them.
Light became a metaphor of dark,
love of hate, joy of sorrow.
With mind opaque Taliesin
balanced the oxymoron of his life.

14
TALIESIN AND THE DARK

I was born before the dark,
And seeing its conception
Understand its nature.
I am myself part of it.

My acts are acts of contrition.

I woke naked in the dark,
Body blazing with pale fire.
My hands weave subtle strains of power,
My sight shines blue as broken sky,

Love and hate abide together in my thought.

I understand the unicorn's song
And my own is of owls and flowers.
I have made my voice of night and time.
My shadow goes before me like a spear.

At sunrise the night bows low.

15
TALIESIN AND MORGAIN

Meeting her eyes the poet laughed.
'You,' he whispered, 'who are near death,
who feel his breath upon your neck,
closer than ever was breath of man,
are on the brink of new things.'

He laughed and the woman fell away
through endless passages of time.
The Poet dreamed away the hours
between age and age; smiling,
he drank the air like a thirst-crazed man.
'I am far,' he whispered, 'from the death
that will come to me only when I call.'

He left the woman with her cold bones
rubbing sparks from the air.
Time followed him closely,
but he could laugh, still.
The woman died.

16
TALIESIN AND THE FLEDGLING DREAM

His fledgling dream
cracked its shell—
smoked out on his breath.

The poet scooped
snow in handsfull
into his mouth.

Chewing and swallowing
his throat constricted
on raw ice.

Thus shriven
he let his song
go free.

It bodied forth
his fledgling dream.

17
TALIESIN THE SALMON

Taliesin is the silver salmon
in the broad-mouthed dish,
the seed in the basket
from the hen's sharp beak.

He comes as he wills
To Gwyddno's weir,
As child from the bag
Or a man from the sea.

Preserver and confessor,
All captivities endures;
Hides within every image
In the Sacred Wood.
He moves the roots before him,
And outstares the eye of day.

All semblances he puts on,
But his true shape is the salmon's;

TALIESIN THE SALMON

He is brother to Dylan*
And his original country
Is the Region of the Summer Stars.

---

* Welsh God of the Sea

18
TALIESIN ALONE

Taliesin walked in the world.
Free, he expressed himself in thoughts that flew
From mind to action like arrows of desire.
Without believing anything but himself—
His own self-possessed truth—
The Poet swept all before him,
Limited the rulers of the empty word.

He sang:
'I too have been shadowed, freedom-curtailed.
Fenced round with dreams, with images.
Naked, duality outlawed, flesh and spirit one
We become destructionless towers
In the centre of being—without echo,
Without bending of truth.
A dream, woven and projected
On a scheme of actuality portrayed.'

The Poet walked alone,
As only those may who have been dead
And seen the destiny of their kind.

He sang:
'To look at a peopled universe
And in a blink sweep all away;
To then put back meaning, truth,
Rejection of the self—mocking or not—
That looks back from a houseless mirror
Blazoned in the maze's heart.
From these constructs comes
A new dream, made real
By the foolish posturer before his gods,
Erected on cardboard thrones.'

This truth the poet saw,
And laughed at its pretension,
Feeling between his hands
The beating of a giant heart.

19
POEM ON TALIESIN'S BIRTHDAY

My words,
jostle in the Vault of Time
seeking entry/exit
from the place of unknowing
into the place of sense and consciousness.

My thoughts,
urgent as spring growth
press through earth
in the silence of knowing,
towards the place of sun and sentience.

My dreams,
dark as old songs,
hasten to the moment
when a voice, in silent space,
will bring forth words
of peace and contemplation.

20
TALIESIN AND THE INSPIRATION OF MOTHER EARTH

Naked, Taliesin lay bound in earth.
He felt himself grow vast.
On his white body the earth lay thick.
He felt its dark hands on his breast.
He neither woke nor dreamed.
His body became a weapon
Piercing the body of mother earth—
Until, with a cry, he was reborn
Cast naked on the frozen earth.
Thus painlessly and through pain,
He harrowed the womb of inspiration.

21
TALIESIN AND THE NOBLE HEAD

Taliesin walked on the hill where the ravens
No longer screamed. Anger transformed him
As he looked where the earth lay turned.
He thought of the Head—the White Head
Of Bran—laid there to watch for the dark;
The skull whose scream would raise the dead
To march against the kingdom's fall.

Clear a speech he heard the voice of Bran.
He remembered the Island and the Tower of Glass.
Once again he heard the voices of the Nine
And saw the mists that curled above the Cauldron's rim.
In the depths of his cold brain he saw
the Red Man from the poisonous lake,
And watched him strike the Dolorous Blow
Deep in the thighs of Lordly Bran.
Remembering, a spark of fire lit his eyes.
He turned away,
Walking like a ghost from the hill.
In silence he went from the King's court.
The Cauldron bubbled in the Castle of the Grail.

22
TALIESIN AND THE STONE OF SEEING

Hunched once more,
under the hard brow of winter
Taliesin spoke the dream aloud:
'No words', he sang, 'Can cause
such truths to pour down
drawn from the edge of winter
into the day's open hand.

Only my belief in the carving
of letters from the Stone of Being
confirms in me the knowledge
of the inner worlds.'

23
TALIESIN'S SONG OF THE SECRETS

I am Taliesin, Divine Child of the Mother,
Who speaks in riddles from the Fountain of Vision.
My words are for those who know
The roots of the trees and the secrets of the earth.
Let me relate how the sun
Shone upon the faces of heroes,
And receive from me the seven secrets
Of my Mother's name.
Three times seven and then three
Were the number of her priestesses;
Two times seven and then two
Where the number of her poets.
Twelve shadows had she and six faces
To watch her children of the night.
Nine were the maidens
Who breathed upon her Cauldron
To keep it from boiling.
Five are the number of her skirts in heaven
And only the God may raise them all.
Four kept watch at the Tower of the Winds.
Two were her progeny except for myself.

But I am Taliesin and I am the first—
The last of the poets to sing her praise:
That my tongue be silvered with moonlight,
That my brow be radiant with song,
That my throat be pure as water,
That my dreams be only of her.

Listen then to my songs.
Understand the poet's secret speech.

24
THE KING'S MIND

The poet crept
in the mind of the king
urging him to find
the truth behind the fires
that danced in his head.

Taliesin, winged, fled
across the dreaming land,
seeking the answer
to the broken things.

He fell, and with him
the dreams of Logres
shattered into fragments
too small to find again.

TALIESIN AND THE BURDEN OF LOVE

The poet walked in the wood alone—
His eyes fearing rumours of Spring,
As buds broke under his gaze.

'How deep the dream runs in me tonight.
I hear the stones talking in the stream bed,
And over me the trees lean together
And talk of the source of all life.
I, who have learned to fear no strength
Greater than time,
Bow before the slightest breeze
Blowing from the mouth of spring.

'Lady, we have met before.
My world is not your world.
My way not yours.
Similar, our journey to the Summer Stars.'

The brightness of day revealed itself.
Bough and leaf trembled on his breath.
Flowers fell from his hands.

Blodeuwedd was reborn
The poet saw the weight of love
Bowing the branches
And fell prey to the vision
Of his own heart—
Pierced by sharp twigs and burning in light.

He saw for a moment everything that had died.
The word opened to the dance of summer.
Darkness lay behind as he bent his neck.

26

TALIESIN AND ARTHUR

Silent, the king's poet stood in the hall of Camelot.
Blind, the Falcons stared on their perches.
The poet said: 'You have broken the bough.
The Apple of Healing is despoiled. Bran's Head
Cries out to empty air; the Kingdom
Falters.'
  Arthur said: 'While I live,
No one but I shall hold the sword of peace;
No one but I let loose the arrow from the string.'

'Other strings there are,' Taliesin answered.
'The song I shall sing is of quest.
Be ready to look your last
On the faces of your knights.
    The Quest
Has no end but for three—and three
Who echo them in the dark labyrinth.
Between these I shall walk, blindfold at need,
Watching the kingdom's life or death.'
    The King stirred

In his chair. The belled feet of falcons jingled.
Already he heard the echo of Mordred's wound.

27
THE FALL OF THE KINGDOM

Quietly and at last the Poet
Took his place in the hierarchic world.
Saw the signs that told him
Time had escaped and the Kingdom founded
Between the King's love and the Queen's desire.

He spoke no word but waited,
Watching the clouds
That massed above the city
Dimming the gleams of gold.
He held a mirror before his face,
Breathed upon its surface,
Clouding it with shadows
Which in the sun shone white.
He sank into reveries in which
The Kingdom was both born and died.

Unheard, the King stood at Camlann
Crying to the dead to rise.
At length the Poet woke from dreaming,

Set out again upon his road
His exact eye recording
Every leaf on the trees he passed.
As though they had been his dreams,
Memory of the Kingdom faded into mist.

28
TALIESIN'S CREED

In the rock, alive,
I would be hewn from it
Like a dream of stone—
Like Merlin, my brother,
In the hidden place.

A feather in bright air
I drift in memory's disguise,
Shadowy as sunlight shaped by sea.
Half in, half out,
I am reborn.

I am in the stone
I am in the wood
I am in the sun
I am in the dancing
I am in all things—

This is my freedom
This my strength

This my journeying
This my discovery
This my self!

29
THE UNICORN

On the green hill, under the thorn tree,
the Unicorn stood like a frozen wave.
Lightning played about its horn,
its hooves danced on grass.

Taliesin stood at the hill's foot,
watched the moon slide out of sight.

Through narrowed eyes he watched the beast—
archetype and symbol under a dark sky.

Each knew the other's strengths and weaknesses,
and the knowledge held them fast.

Then, for a heartbeat, Poet and beast were fused,
man-unicorn, white maned and horned.

Then each was back in his own flesh,
having borrowed something of the other.

In silence the Poet turned away.
The hill resounded to the beat of soundless hooves.

TALIESIN AND THE NIGHT HAWK

At moonrise Taliesin heard the Night Hawk scream.
From the Hill where the beacon flared,
He watched its fire in the green-lit sky,
Tracing patterns above the walls of the sleeping caer.
Secret and silent he walked the old trackways,
Following their pattern through the winding dark.

Shadows closed fast around him on the wind,
And against them he sang white words.
Shards of light broke round his head.
He sang—his words were as flames that burned the air.
He waited, watching for an answer in the East,
And heard the distant scream of a Peacock
In the gardens of the King's palace at Camelot,
Until a spear of light, hawk-forgotten,
Showed above the world's dark edge.

Unaware of circling darkness, the City stirred.
The poet smiled at its innocent life,
Thought of its good, remembered its evil.

Weighing these thoughts he wondered
How long before he would be called again
To test his song against the Night Hawk's screech,
Where it hung, dazed by sun, above unseeing heads.

THE RECONCILIATION OF OPPOSITES

I am the reconciler.
I hold the opposites in either hand
And, without letting them approach,
Allow them to commingle.
In the moment of reconciliation

I am the center,
The tree at the storm's heart,
The reflection of true night,
An alembic of light and dark.

As the waves of silence rise,
The land shudders—
But the blow never falls.
Held back by their measured strokes,
All time teeters,
Falls from my steady hand
Like grains of winnowed wheat.

My words themselves
Are a balance and a blending

Of wisdom and folly.
I have seen to the heart
Of the roseate Grail;
Where the Cauldron gleams
I have drunk.

Madness is not my measure.
Love is now my tomb.

32
THE SONG OF THE WIND

Taliesin heard the roaring of the wind.
He listened to its dark iron voice.
From the trees' shelter he walked with it
As it led him by hill and stream,
Lent him wings to leap the land.

Beyond the dark hills, by trembling walls,
Walking with the wind's wisdom,
Taliesin sang through Logres,
Sang the wild songs of death and renewal,
Went out upon the shores and called the waves,
Gave back song for song from the Singing Head,
And in the wind knew matchless wisdom for his own.

33
THE LOST LIGHT

Cold and smooth as polished bone
the Dream flew in the poet's head.
He seized at the edge of meaning
bobbing on the rim of his thought;
he heard, like a distant cry of birds,
the echoed memory of his truth.
Found before the birth of time.

Darkly he walked on the hills' back
piping like a hedgefull of birds.
Spread his arms like wings
and caught the sun between them.
Squeezing it in his two hands,
he tossed it back into the sky,
went laughing on his way.

34
IN WINTER'S SHADOW

Under the brow of winter
Taliesin stood,
Feeling, in head and heart,
The tremor of ice-kept streams.
His eyes were the color of ice.

Watching, from sheltering stones,
He felt, in hands and feet,
The pain of snow-bound boughs.
His eyes were the color of frost.
Then, as snow flowed from him,
His voice thawed.
He barked like a fox at midnight,
Sang with the waters' release.
His eyes were the color of spray.

35

THE RAID ON ANNWN

— I —

The acorn cup is filled with blood
And starlight trembles
In the mirror of Annwn.

Downward the Director of Toil
Led us, and we followed,
Into the shadow of the shadow,
And beyond, into
The full weight of Winter,
Iron armor of ice
That kept us slow.

Afloat on the Dragon-raft
We approached sunset, the tower
Where night's agents flamed.
We followed our lord
To the night of midnight
Where even Time's sickness
Can be cured.

THE RAID ON ANNWN

— II —

Ocean showed us the way
towards sun and after-sun.

Trailing our bow through light
the way fell into mid-world.

Mirrored by stars we watched
the slow revolving of spheres.

At last, in comprehension,
not lost, we spoke the Name.

It sang, swordlike,
in the dark. Waking
In the mouth of Annwn
To the lap of water and the creak of oars.

— III —

What wind blows in Annwn?
How are the sails of Prydwen filled?
On the Dragon's breath we sailed
Towards the rim of the world.
Beneath the head of the Beast
Were stars for scales . . .
The clatter of his breath
Rang in our ears;
Our eyes, filled with shadows,
Mirrored stars.

The maze dissolved
In shards of sun;
And water drew back

From the lip of shore.
Sailing in, the lantern
Swayed in the wind;
Returning, the flame
Stands still as a spear.

36

TALIESIN'S SONG OF THE APOTHEOSIS OF BRITAIN

I am the owl whose blood
Drained through the earth
Where the Stone of Gronw fell,
Shivered by a single spear.
I am the raven who saw
The towers of Caer Siddi fall,
Who watched the smoke curl up
From Druid fires on Wansdyke Hill.
Last, I am the poet-sage
Who saw the Age of Man arrive,
And danced on Glastonbury's winter hill
As the Serpent slid from view;
Who saw the warrior Michael fall,
And heard the Dragon singing to its hoard.

In moonlight I gave witness
to the rites of Arthur's passing in the barge;
And sang the ancient stones to rest
Amid the clanging echoes of Craig Dhu—
Watching all the while, in misted dawn
The slow sad birth of day

From Silbury's burning hill.

Now I have come to rest at last,
And stretch forth my hand to grasp
The sleeping Giant's staff;
While in Merlin's grove, the head of Bran
Sings Caer Siddi into silvered dust,
And moonlight stains the ancient ways
That lead to the Dragon's eye.
The White Horse of the downs gets up,
And goes to meet the mourning Queen,
Whose dreams become my truth again
As night rolls back before new day.

37
TALIESIN SINGS THE HEROES

I remember the Hall of Heimdall
Where smoke rose from the hearth-place;
I remember also the gold-gift,
Red metal glinting in the fire-glow—
And through all ways I go alone.

I remember the castles of stone
That stood out grey and black upon the land
Where banners drooped and pennons
Whipped in the wind that does not change—
And through all ways I go alone.

I remember how it was when the Red Man
Flung his Holly twig at Baldur,
Who was also Bendeigvran,
Whose singing head we buried in White Mount—
And through all ways I go alone.

I remember how the hunt drove on
Through still wild forests
In quest of the white beast, unicorn or stag;

And how we could not catch them ever—
And through all ways I go alone

I remember the pale eyed shapes
That rose in darkness from the Barrow-mounds;
Who would not lie in peace or restfulness
While their despoilers went unchained—
And through all darknesses I go alone.

I remember the words of Myrddin,
Who came from the sea with *awen* in his eyes;
Who walks no longer by the shore
But lies through ages hidden in the earth—
And through all ages I go alone.

I remember when the Wolf was chained
And why the Wanderer swapped his eye,
And after, wore the Hat of Darkness—
The colour, anciently, of wisdom—
and through all ways I go alone.

I remember who it was that struck the blow
Which cracked the Grey King's helm;
Who after, sailed for Apple Isle,
With three dark women at his side—
And through all seasons I go alone.

I remember the wood where the Last Prince went,
Pursuing the final Dragon of the West,
To whom the two White Beasts came walking
To lay him in his grave of stone—
And through all deaths I go alone

I remember who went searching
for the Cauldron and the Grail,

And what they found, and where,
And who came back to tell of it—
And on all quests I go alone.

I remember in the stillness
How the horns were wound for Balin,
who knew he was their lawful prey
But laughed, and took the Middle Road—
And on all roads I go alone.

I remember still the Kings and Princes,
The Heroes and the Lordly Knights,
The swords and rings and talismans
Of ages in the dust—
And through that dust I go alone.

38
THE VOICES IN THE GRASS

Taliesin walked where the gray stones rose.
The dry susurration of grass from every side
Sang in the poet's ears as he walked
Recalling the glory of the place whose bones lay bare.
Softly, as the sun beat down,
he heard the Voice of the grass whispering
broken syllables of forgotten speech.
Behind the murmur he heard one voice say:
'Taliesin: Poet, watcher under moon and sun,
Walks where the gray stones once stood tall,
Listens to the voices in the Summer grass,
Remembers the lost time he knew between the walls,
Scents again the perfume of a full-blown rose . . .
Taliesin: Poet, watcher under sun and moon,
Walks where the dry stones . . .'
Shrill, the poet
Whistled in the dry air, halting in its tracks
The wild life of the place—while the grass
For a moment seemed to still,
And the Voice he knew as echoing his own
Fell silent among the tumbled stones of Camelot.

39
TALIESIN AND THE SILENCE OF WINTER

Silence crawled across the snowfields.
It lapped against the walls of the castle.
Pale wintry sunlight flashed silver
From the branches of trees
And the frozen stems of grass
That rattled together like naked finger joints.
The Poet stood on a snow-lipped parapet,
Stared towards hills where something gleamed.
Behind him, on the castle's further side,
A black river ran, from which arose
Cold coils of mist, so that the water
Seemed to smoke, breathing out on the sharp air.
Waiting, he listened to the silence,
Felt it approach along the ground like a drowning wave.

Only where he stood was there still life.
His face seemed dead,
Yet his lips moved and his eyes saw...
        Then,
His fingers flew, flashed white
On the gray walls, and from his lips, words poured...

In answer to his summons
The light that moved across the waste
Warmed and grew golden suddenly.
Out of the still and burning sky
Birdsong fell.
                Beyond his sight a bird flew,
Let fall a feather that floated to rest
At his feet...
                At length he looked down,
Fell silent and grew still again.
Slowly the silence drew back.
The black waters of the river received it.
And with a sound like indrawn breath,
Sounds of nearing Spring returned.
On the far hills the silver quivered.
A single speck flashed momentary gold.

40
TALIESIN AND THE RAVEN

Raven has transformed me.
In feather-black I dance
In cloak of dust I dance
In black-wing-rags, I dance.

Raven has remade me.
I see with his eyes
I sense with his senses
I gabble with his beak.

Raven has taken me.
I am shaken by his knowing
By a wisdom older than rock,
By a strength pure as water

By his gift of perception
By his gift of laughter
By his gift of joy.

41
TALIESIN AND THE SONG OF THE QUEST

Eyes like spears had Taliesin.
From his chair at the head of the hall
He watched gravely the play of the knights.
Once wine had been drunk and food consumed
He laid hands to his wondrous harp-strings
And struck from them a song of wisdom.
In the midst of the carousal he made silence,
And laid forth a song of the subtle Goddess,
Naming her the Friend of Life, and Huntress of the Wood.

To the hushed and waiting throng
He sang the beginning of the Quest.
They heard his words in silence, the famous Bard;
And some smiled in wonder at his song—
They who did not know,
Of his journey to Caer Sidi where
He heard songs of the Noble Head
That told how the Kingdom would fall.

All the while, in the hall of Arthur,
He made songs of warning that went unheard.

Not wise the one who
Scorns the words of a poet
Versed in the wisdom of the Wood,
Whose initiation was before recorded time,
Whose strength was as fire in the blood.

42
TALIESIN AND THE LAKE OF VISION

In the high places of the land
the song of the poet continues
opening its unequalled orisons
to all who listen, beating down
on the mirrored lake of dreams.

Here, the King's Poet,
Taliesin of the Radiant Brow
utters a new blessing:
that all who seek find,
that all who find, offer
the diverse strands of their wisdom—
whether formed at the Cauldron's rim
or the inward-beating heart.

The poet's message rings in the soul's cage
like a bright bird, caught
in the chiming moment,
offers a truth that echoes
in the darkest corners,
in the highest-dreaming spires

of the blessed land.

With him, we come to the edge;
remembering all he has given,
We descend to a place
of newly turned earth,
where the fires are banked
and the Cauldron feeds
soul and heart and mind.

43
TALIESIN ENTERS THE WOOD

The Wood is a dark and silent place
where I am able, at last, to understand,
set in place all the fragments of knowledge
which together make a perfect whole.

I came here through uncharted ways,
roads known only to those whose search
leads them deeper into the resounding dark
in which their truth lies hidden.

Unwilling almost from the start,
and certainly neither happy or at peace,
they who walked this way had nothing
except the guidance of a certain goal.

Now I am able to see the completed pattern,
to judge for myself where I belong.
How much of the truth is bearable
I shall not know until the coming day.

44
THE BATTLES OF
LIGHT AND DARK

Long have I sought to understand
the war between light and dark.
Always I have seen
darkness settle on the walls
of Camelot the Golden—
dimming its glow.
Then, each morning, watched this
thrown off by the rising of the sun.

Also, I have seen
a darkness in all men,
that rises out of them
to paint a dark shadow
across the land.
Sometimes this is dispelled
by strength of will
to carry out the acts of truth.
that all men carry within.

Wisdom and the sovereign glance
sustain me. The bitter taste

of the Cauldron's brew
rises like bile in my throat—
and I am again transformed.

The struggle may have no end,
and much that I see tells me
this is an all too familiar charge.
Yet, when I hear the call of birds
from the highest trees in the Golden Wood
my heart grows strong again
and the rhythms of song
stir within me.

I am Taliesin.
Bearer of both light and dark.

45
TALIESIN AND THE TREE

Time out of mind Taliesin watched the tree,
And in a moment moved to enter its heart.
Dreaming there through the seasons,
He felt the summer fade with an exhausted sigh.

Wind among the grey boughs
Changed its roaring to a song;
Leaning into it, he laughed,
'Til it parched both lips and throat.

Autumn fell away behind him,
Left a gleam of poet's gold beneath every hedge.
All winter he watched the snowfields,
Saw the sun burn down and the moon conquer.

Dreaming, he woke to the dance of spring.
Having learned all he might
he went singing away.
In sunlight the tree mourned his song.

46
TALIESIN SINGS OF HIS KNOWLEDGE

Once I knew
Everything there was to know:
In a moment of burning ecstasy
I became transformed,
Knew every rock and tree
Bird, animal, and fish,
And, in a twinkling,
Perceived all meanings to be one.

Then, in just as swift a moment,
From lightnings to returning dark,
I forgot all I had learned.
It was as though, where I had beheld
Only unities, now I beheld,
Only the fragmented moieties
Which once were whole.

Since then, long years of seeking,
Of striving to recover the fragments
Through which I might, somehow,
Put back the broken littoral

TALIESIN SINGS OF HIS KNOWLEDGE

Into that same whole
Which is eternal
And does not change.
Only I have changed, become
Frozen in time and space.

Now I look back
At the past and push
The fragments into new patterns,
Eternally hoping to find
Their true relationship,
So that the fire of creation
Might be kindled
In my bones.

47
TALIESIN: THE POET'S EYE

I am the bird that shone above the water; that sang
down the bright ways leading to and from the Moon.
Did you not hear my song as you rode your horse-like symbol
with its fragile fragrant horn and hoofs
that left no prints in the sand?

I have flown in the aisles of the silent Wood and have dared
to fling my song at the darkened tangled brakes that held
fast to their captives. There a thousand lovers wept at their fate;
I have forgotten the number of times I have died for those tears.

Numberless the times I have entered
the Castle on its dreaming hill;
Have seen its walls for the lies they became,
and watched the Glass Tower
on its island of song, which alone
could understand its captives' moan.
And no one now remembers this, but she who sang, once:

'Sweet bird, gentle songster, the gift of your presence is good';
and from those words, grew wings herself—to fly the Castle,

depart the Wood. Her face continues to haunt me,
though I cannot love, and my way lies
beyond where she could go.

The pathways of the Moon have called me out of life;
the questions I have asked so often without hope,
remain unanswered, quivering back
from the moving water—and as I look down I can see
no reflection there but the Moon. Call *that* the poet's eye.

48
TALIESIN'S QUEST

— I —

In a wood heavy with violets
I wandered in search of the star
I had marked in its passage
Down the sky. But the trees
Were dark, kept their secrets
In heavy silence, hung down
Their crabbed boughs,
Writhed their thick roots,
Moaned to themselves, tormentedly.

— II —

On a lake of moon-broken water
I sailed in search of the light
I had seen gleaming
Through torn cloud-wrack
Above the mountain's eye.
But the wind knifed through me
As though it would sever soul from body,

And the water was too dark
To hold my reflection.

— III —

In a deep-delved cave
I sought the twisted shadow
I had marked in torchlight
Where it played on crystal walls,
Reflecting the faces of those
Who had hunted there before.
But the torchlight flickered
And went out, and having not
The noctule sight of those
Who went before, I failed to see
The water where the dark wood lay.

49
TALIESIN'S MADNESS

The poet crept
in the mind of the king
urging him to find
the truth behind the fires
that danced in his head.

Taliesin, winged, fled
across the dreaming land
seeking answers
to the broken things.

He fell, and with him
the dream of Logres
shattered into fragments
too small to find again.

50
SONG OF THE GRAIL-LORD

I sing of the stranger who is Lord of the Grail.
Pushing against the clouded walls of the world.
The night trembles and shakes as he moves,

Dark centres shift and merge in the darkness of the Wood.
Between the twisted shapes of memory, twilight
Rises like a cloud of dust—the morning falls choked and dead.

Power holds me caught in a net of spider-webs
Drawing me towards the lip of the abyss.
I cry, but my cry goes unheard on the dizzy edge.

A moist wind drags at the mind's limit,
And the form I wear begins to melt,
Trickling like smoke in the grey air.

Irresistibly drawn I move towards the dark
Knowing as I do that the dark itself
Draws nearer to a darker night.

I forget, and forget again as the shapes change,

Forget that I am drawn in a moving urge,
A desire to return to the flame of creation.

I sing of the lord who is master of the Grail,
Trusting that I move
Outward from the darkness of my world,

To learn again the secrets of Caer Siddi.

TALIESIN TO THE CROWS

First in autumn,
through spring
into summer—
mix-matched seasons
and only winter left—
I came adrift
in a sea of memory
and sank
in a sudden chill
that swept the waves.

Borne under
I lay in the deep,
bosomed in peace,
where only the
sound of singing
pierced
the waves' sad thunder.

And now, at rest
(they say),

I turn and master
the tides that flow
over and under,
over and under
this deep-delved hollow
filled with late-blooming fire—

that slow, sad harvest,
pressed by necessity,
into the shape
of a winter dream.

TALIESIN'S SONG OF THE RETURNING

— I —

They have all gone, lamenting, under the hills,
lamenting for their Lord who is lost;
hidden in the waste where the earth dries up
to the death of the Grailless lands.

They have all gone under, into the raths
that are silent now, shut fast as the soul,
prisoned like their Lord under lands of ice.

Mabon is lost and all is lost till the thaw
when the ice-breath shakes on the sickened land
and the King is set free from his boundless chains.

They have all gone, lamenting, under the land
to the place where the mothers of the race are born;
where the myths of the Grailless lands are born
to be spoken in whispers in the lightless realm.

— II —

He comes, the one who frees the waters
and in his train spring comes—
the child of Modron reigning in splendour.

Bright as that light on the Radiant Brow
he stands at the aeon-gated City on the hill—
with bow and quiver at his back.

And they who were gone, lamenting, lamenting
come forth to dance in the morning light;
and the light falls long on the Grailless lands
till the trees are adrift in leaves of light.

Mabon, Mabon, we call you again
free us from the prison of the iron gates,
free us again from winter's bite.

Mabon, Mabon, will call to you once more
thrice we call you back through the open door
to dance on the grass at the water's gate.

For they who lamented under the hills
return now with you to dance thereon;
and the children of the raths come forth in the wind
that all that was sorrow is now joyful again.

And the sunlight dances in the Grailless lands
and the moonlight flickers on the Grailless lands
since Mabon son of Modron came out of the hills.

53
TALIESIN IN THE MOMENT

Hunched under the iron brow of winter
The Poet carved the words
in the unhewn arch—
driven far into night
but seeking a glimpse
of the hallowed thing.

Finding the moment true
he moved forth in today
watching the tumbling birds
play in the hollows of the wind.

54
TALIESIN THE SHAMAN

Half in
half out of the worlds
I'm caught
like a shadow
cut from its source
dreaming
dreaming
shifting shape

Into
out of the worlds
I dance
like a candle-flame
caught
by the wind

I'm half dream
half real
what am I?
that the wind knows

that the moon knows
that the earth knows

that they never tell!

TALIESIN & THE SONG OF TRADITION

In the high places of the Land
Tradition's song continues,
Offering its unequalled orison
To all who listen,
beating down on the mirrored lake of dreams.

Here, the King's poet,
Taliesin of the Radiant Brow,
Utters a new blessing:
That all who seek,
That all who find,
May discover their wisdom,
Whether at the Cauldron's rim
Or from the inward beating heart.

The poet's message
Flutters in the soul's cage
Like a bright bird;
The truth he utters
Echoes in the darkest corners,
Rings out from the highest-dreaming-spires

In the bright land.

With him, we come to the edge;
Remembering all he has given
We descend to a place
Of new-turned earth.

56

TALIESIN'S LAMENT FOR LLACHEU THE KING'S SON

How sad with me how sad!
The King's son, Llacheu,
Has lost his light in the dark of the Wood.
Before him rose the unmanifest,
the evil of the Grail of night.
The battle raged in the dream of light -
the bright Prince returned no more.

Deep is the Woodside where he lies.
my sorrow for the passing of my Lord!
Llacheu, the King's son, of noble brow,
sleeps in the shadow of the Wood of Death.
Before him in the halls of dream,
the unmanifest evil wove,
and and glitter of battling blades
strove with the night of stars.
Now ravens croak where the bright one rode
and light is quenched in Camelot.

57
TALIESIN SINGS THE MYSTERIES

Taliesin sang:
'There have been great mysteries where I was.'
He felt the dark heart of the world beat in his brain.
He held out his hand and the trees woke to a wind-song.
He touched the earth and summer came.
He knew the secrets of the mountain's roots.
He had been everywhere and done everything
And knew all answers.
All the sorrows of the world were his,
And in his own heart sorrow dwelled.

All he once had loved were gone.
He felt himself alone and longed
To follow where they led.
He knew the mysteries of death and life.
Choosing his own way
As he walked between tall gates,
He sang of all births and deaths;
Both newborn and rising things replied.
He sang the great Mysteries—

And all who heard him
Understood the secrets of his holy voice.

58
TALIESIN ANSWERS THE CRITICS

I stand witness
to blind faces.

My song is of rivers,
my song is of stars.

I am the centre
yet touch the peripheral.

My thought is inclusive,
embracing time.

I sing the myths continually,
that are of all worlds.

My view will be total
at the beginning of night's end.

59
A SONG OF THE EMPIRE

(for Charles Williams)

Between the pages of the Wood, the stages
of the Kingdom rise. Masked is the glory;
the story, told. We, who stand at the gate,
wait but the word, the gesture
complete from the hands of the Emperor
who stands at the head of the turning stair.

The masks of the Empire remain;
they train the dream
to spell out the facts of the acts
of Rome. Until the dreams
of the Company turn
again to the journey,
under the auspices of the Summer Stars,
back to the faces of Camelot and Carbonek.

A SONG OF THE EMPIRE

Heard in the occiput of Logres
the word of the mage extends
forward and downward into the world
which, having heard, lets fall
the dream and the vision of transfigured Time.
There, caught up, transformed, the mirrors
turn and burn and shine
into the darkness beyond the World.

Shapes of longing and belonging
to the patterns of the Acts of Being
found in the round archives
of the state of things-to-be,
shadow forth the making of earth.
Taliesin saw, in the shadow,
a new beginning, the beasts and the burdens
turned to gifts in the journey of the Wood and the World.
When desire flamed in the ire of being
light glowed on the face of the beloved;
The King's poet merged the dreams that urged
a fruitful union of spirit and flesh.

Thus we are come, at last, past
the gate of the Wood, under the shadow
of Camelot in the Empire's shape
to the mysteries of the Graal;
the Cup flames in the heart and the mind;
the subtle changes of King and kind
Shapes of soul in the flesh of Broceliande.

The shadow of the Graal, the Cup
that is sought and the Cup that seeks
brought by the hands of the Holy Spirit
into the lands of human endeavour
showed by its light where Arthur reigned,

where the Table stood
as the Song of Logres echoed in the Wood,
and all that was to be was told
in the manner of song, in the matter of mind.

In the habit of truth
the gesture of acceptance pulls us,
to adore the rule, mounts
through the founts and funnels,
the vessels of the realms of blood,
and sings, springs in our hearts,
heads, souls, the song of the King's Poet's joy.
Welcomed in the sanctity of space
the Queen blends, sends forth
her blessing. All time trembles.
Logres comes again, thrusting
through the trusting gate of the soul.

We come to the light of the Graal;
are changed, unmade,
woefully arrayed; are caught
up in the heavenly moment,
the general movement of all things
towards the infinite and perfect whole.

In a high chamber, the King trembled,
saw before him the cherubim flame.
Joy burned away his last forgetting
as he moved to be one with the Company's infinite heart.
Hope leapt in the hearts and heads
of the Seekers of Logres;
truth burned in the mind
like an incandescent cloud;

the trees bowed their heads
as the Hands deployed
the mysteries and joys
of the true act the Seekers enjoined.

The Graal sang from the depths of space
an ancient and holy blessing
that rang in the Hallows of the Kingdom's heart.

60
BEFORE CAMLANN

In the King's court
A single lantern burned,
Holding back the dark.
Taliesin, standing above the gate,
saw the small gleam
And breathed out the words:
'As long as the light burns
Memory enfolds us, truth is held
by the hands of both
The infinite and the earthly Lords.'
The King turned, restless in his bed,
As though he felt the words,
Understood their meaning.
Elsewhere, Lancelot, burning
With his own dark light,
Sweated out the dream
He carried eternally within.
Gawain, the blaze of his fires
Dimmed by the darkness,
Paced in his room,
Swearing vengeance for the death

Of Gareth in the crowded yard.
All these, and the rest,
The Golden courtiers of the Golden court,
Slept or woke or waited.
Only the King's poet, wakeful, held the gate
And breathed out his greatest fear:
'If all fails tomorrow,
The dream must still survive.'
His words, like bright birds, flew
From the gates and outward,
Over the darkened land. Distant,
The Moon woke, escaping the cover
Of cloud and, swollen with portent,
Swept across a world,
Yet unprepared for war.

61
TALIESIN AND THE NYMPH

In the light of Spring I came to the Wood again,
Rested a while by the Fountain, listening to its voice.
My eyelids drooped, and forgetting the Spring
Of Vision, saw in the fountain the face of a Nymph.

I felt myself caught in a timeless net,
My thoughts playful and out of touch with time;
Then I remembered Merlin, eclipsed in the earth,
And my eyes, clouded for that moment, grew clear again.

My voice found new power as I sang of love,
Played dark against light and made them one.
I swept the shadows from darkened minds,
Brought light into hearts where unfulfillment lay.

In the Wood, and in the King's palace,
A new dream flowered from strong roots.
Touching the Nymph's starred breasts with fire
I challenged where I had bowed and smiled.

TALIESIN AND THE NYMPH

My laughter rang clear in the silent Wood
The Night Hawk and the Shadows reeled.
Love was at my fingers—
Spelled out it became transformed.

62
TALIESIN'S DAEMON

Wading to his knees in icy water
Taliesin cursed the air he breathed,
watched his laughing daemon
as she made her way
quite calmly to the riverbank.

Once there, he laughed also,
seeing the lunacy of life
which led him to such things.

63
TALIESIN AND THE MINGLED WORLDS OF CHRIST

Under green trees and red Taliesin walked.
He bent his head above the river, seeking the salmon's wisdom.
He looked to where the branches scraped against the sky:
but the eagle, like the fish, offered him no words.
'I exist,' the poet said, 'and all this too.
The knowledge of stalk and stem,
of blood and flower, of branch, are mine.
Yet still my knowledge fails, and there is
still no answer to the oldest riddle of all.'
He walked again, into silence, onto snow-enfolded ground.
'This Christ men follow. I have known his ways
under different suns; yet not seen his miracles.
Now they are saying he lays claim to all that is—
more than Gwydion, or the White Queen herself,
and I see the shadow of his Tree grown long.
I have sought the truth as a poet
and nowhere been touched as by the glowing pattern
I read in the shadows of water and leaf—
voices in the grass, the gleam of ripened corn,
the flash of a gull's wing and the cry of the sea against rocks;
the eternal susurrus of moving stones.

These have taught me the things Ceridwen could not,
enough to keep Merlin's flame steady in my mind,
but not to outshine the pearl-light at the Cauldron's rim.
Now Arthur's men go looking for something they will not find
and I must take my flesh and bones
through the cold stones of winter
to rediscover Bran's gift of blood.
In blood the truth will be dissolved—
this much at least I know.
I, Taliesin, who never asked a question
I could not answer, find myself outfoxed.'
His words were like a song in the silent Wood;
tree and flower, bird and beast, heard his words.
In Sarras, City of the Grail
the Mystery prepared itself for Galahad,
and in the midst of bread and wine
Bran's sacrifice, the child of God,
the age-hoar poet's longing for a dream of truth
entered one into the other, and fused.
Before the eyes of Taliesin, Sun's light and Moon's light mixed.

64
TALIESIN SEES THE LOVERS PASS

In the King's Chair, far above Camelot,
The Poet sat.
He watched the turning of time
and the shaping of life in the kingdom.
His heart went out to the sorrowful ones,
the lovers who sought for recognition
beyond the Table.
The women too he saw and sorrowed for,
The Queen's shadow wavering
Like the flame of a candle
Caught by a passing draft of air.
The broken-hearted lovers, Tristan and Isolde,
drifted in their silken barge
into the drowned world of Avalon.
Elaine of Carbonek rested in her barge,
grasping her last words to Lancelot in her dead hand.
'I stand at the junction of love and no love'
The poet sang. 'Both are offered freely
To those in need.'
The voice of Merlin drifted back:
'Now you have seen the ways that interplay

and are woven and unwoven in the Great Wood.
All truth now lies before you.
Sent through the gate of love.
You have but to reach out.'
A tear traced its track down the Poet's cheek.
Whether for others or himself he could not say.

65
TALIESIN ON THE THIRTEENTH STAIR

Taliesin rose to the thirteenth stair
And turning, saw the Kingdom
Spread out before him. There,
He saw the pattern of the kingly shadow
The light of the Grail in Sarras lodged
While in the east lay the shape
Of Broceliande, the Great Wood that held
The Mystery in its roots
and sent the message of the Cup
Through the branched pathways
Between Camelot and Carbonek.
He listened then, and heard the voice
Of Glatisant* rising above the stones,
and where he stood the Poet saw
The Stone of Merlin's father fly
Across the Venetian city walls.
'What now?' he asked in silence,
and heard in return, the voice of Merlin:
'You are set free to walk the paths

---

* The Questing Beast

I have carved out of the kingdom;
They will lead you to the spiritual place,
where all things meet;
and there shall be remembered
all those who see the vision of the Table,
Before it is broken by Mordred's need
His greed for vengeance
and desire for the queen.

'Go then, poet, and sing the truth
That I might have written had I not
Been taken to this other place.
That you, who understand
the song of the Wood and drink
from the Silver Spring of faery,
Shall tell it yet, as you
journey to the Summer Stars.'

THE SONG OF THE WIND

Taliesin heard the roaring of the wind.
He listened to its dark iron voice.
From the trees' shelter he walked with it
As it led him by hill and stream,
Lent him wings to leap the land.

Beyond the dark hills, by trembling walls,
Walking with the wind's wisdom,
Taliesin sang through Logres,
Sang the wild songs of death and renewal,
Went out upon the shores and called the waves,
Gave back song for song from the Singing Head,
And in the wind knew matchless wisdom for his own.

67
TALIESIN DREAMS

In the high places of the land
the song continues
offering its unequal orison
to all who listen,
beating down on the mirrored lake of dreams.

Here the king's poet,
Taliesin of the Radiant Brow,
utters a new blessing:
that all who seek
that all who find
may discover their wisdom
whether from the Cauldron's rim
or the inward beating heart.

The poet's message
rings in the soul's cage
like a bright bird;
the truth he utters
echoes in the darkest corners
and rings from the highest-dreaming

spires in the land.

With him, we come to the edge,
remembering all he has given
we descend to a place
of fresh-turned earth.

68
TALIESIN AT THE WEIR

Taliesin, carried on the swift waters, sang:
'You proclaim me master of tideless currents,
Child to the daughter of unknowable love,
A light riding down to the waiting dark.'

Knowledge breathed out from the Poet's lips.
The waters grew wilder before the dawn.
At last, he came to Elffin's weir,
Bearing on his brow the moon's cold light.

69
AT THE WEIR AGAIN

Sunlight stretched tight over rock,
Rock scraping the skull, the tongue,
The poet's hands; the shock
Of light recalling songs sung.

Gray water smooth between reaches
Where pale winds rattle reeds at the bank;
He who learned what the dream teaches
Laughed as the bright flame sank.

70
THE RETURN OF TALIESIN

In the broken, roofless hall of stone
The King's Poet swung down from his horse.
He walked its length to find his chair
And sat in its familiar curve again.
He raised his eyes to the sky
Which now was the only banner—
And saw how the stars shone through
The gentle blue of day.

At his summons
Phantoms of the mist arose
To wind in grey procession
Through the hall.

At length, when all
Had passed, Taliesin stood.
In a snap of radiant fingers
He threw down and scattered
The last stones.

71

TALIESIN AND THE WORLD

Taliesin, grown old but with mind untouched,
Sat listening to the murmur of the wind.
He remembered moments of his life:
'I have explored the meanings of things
By way of things as they are found.
Rock, stream, tree, bird and beast,
Fish and fowl have instructed me.
For the realities are what we can see—
Everywhere the perfect truth of being
Flashing back from sunlit leaves,
Speaks from the murmuring stream,
Cries out from the birth and death of creation.
Always the great moments thrust themselves
Outward from the inner soul.
I have striven to become part of everything
And to interpret what I saw.'
The poet remained where he was
But his mind, no longer burdened
By thoughts of Kingdom or Quest,
Flew free, mingling at last as he had longed,
With the forces of rock, earth, water and air.

72
A CHOSEN DEATH

Taliesin heard the roaring of the wind.
He listened to its dark iron voice
And from the sheltering trees walked with it
As it led him, by hill and stream,
Lent him wings to leap the land.

He sang: 'I have seen stones full
the glass break, the sky gashed crimson.
Now I ask that the Tree should remain a tree,
In flower of blossom and leaf—
But no more than that;
And I accept the answer
Inherent in the grain of sand—
Containing as it does
The sound and complexity of song.
Rejecting omniscience,
I walk stumbling into night,
Retaining an awareness of day,
The ability to move forward
Into a pattern more complex than comprehension
In which I shall find my root.'

A CHOSEN DEATH

Cold and smooth as polished bone
The words flew in the Poet's brain.
He seized at the edge of meaning
Bobbing at the rim of his mind
And heard, like a distant cry of birds,
The echoed meaning of his truth.
Beyond the dark hills, by trembling walls,
Walking with the wind's secret wisdom
Taliesin sang through Logres;
Sang the wild songs of birth and dying,
Went out on the shore and called the waves,
Gave back song for song to the Singing Head,
And in the wind knew matchless wisdom for his own.
Darkly he walked in the chastened land
Dreams crunching beneath his feet
Like frost-crisped grass.
In his ears the heavens resounded
With the shrill crying of swallows.
On every side spring unfolded and unfurled.
Taliesin spread his arms like wings
And caught the Sun between his hands—
Laughing tossed it back into the sky,
And with a smile of pure joy, pure sorrow,
Walked to meet his chosen death.

73
THE LAST OF THE WANDERERS

(An Epilogue for Taliesin)

The whitest of the Wanderers—
Where is he?
Into what darkness gone
Or by what light illumined?
Does he sleep yet?
Under the split rock
Has he found rest?
Have his fingers
Lost any of their skill?
And has he found at last
A last song to sing?
Tell me, muse-wife,
Consort-queen of Heaven
Have you heard of him
anywhere among your hills?
In rath, or palace,
Or great-walled dwelling place,
Has his name hung in the air?
His voice swept the strings of the wind?

THE LAST OF THE WANDERERS

Long years there are between us—
An age since he went away,
the last of the White Wanderers.
Can you tell nothing of him?
Wielder of the wisdom sceptre,
Have you not anywhere heard
The sound of his footfall over the grass?
The sound of his breath on the cold air?
The sound of his laughter in the riverbed?
The sound of his voice after birdsong?
Have you not heard?
The last of the White Wanderers—
The very last—
If no one remembers him but I
Who will remember him at all?
He is the last
And he is gone
Nor can I say
Where he is gone.

FURTHER READING

Taliesin: The Last Celtic Shaman by John Matthews (Inner Traditions, 2002)

Song of Taliesin by John Matthews (Quest Books, 2001)

The Book of Taliesin, translated by Gwenyth Lewis and Rowan Williams (Penguin Books, 2020)

The Arthurian Poems of Charles Williams: Including Taliessin Through Logres and The Region of the Summer Stars with Other Poems, ed. Grevel Lindop and John Matthews (Apocryphile Press, 2022)

Taliesin's Map: The Comparative Guide to Celtic Mythology by J. Dolan (Privately Printed, 2022)

www.ingramcontent.com/pod-product-compliance
Lightning Source LLC
Chambersburg PA
CBHW030221170426
43194CB00007BA/820